The Statue of Liberty

Introducing Primary Sources

by Tamra B. Orr

CAPSTONE PRESS
a capstone imprint

Little Explorer is published by Capstone Press,
1710 Roe Crest Drive, North Mankato, Minnesota 56003
www.mycapstone.com

The name of the Smithsonian Institution and the sunburst logo are registered trademarks of the
Smithsonian Institution. For more information, please visit www.si.edu.

Library of Congress Cataloging-in-Publication Data
Orr, Tamra.
The Statue of Liberty : introducing primary sources / by Tamra B. Orr.
pages cm. — (Smithsonian little explorer. Introducing primary sources)
Includes bibliographical references and index.
Summary: "Introduces young readers to primary sources related to the Statue of Liberty"— Provided
by publisher.
ISBN 978-1-4914-8223-0 (library binding)
ISBN 978-1-4914-8607-8 (paperback)
ISBN 978-1-4914-8613-9 (eBook PDF)
1. Statue of Liberty (New York, N.Y.)—Juvenile literature. 2. New York (N.Y.)—Buildings, structures,
etc.—Juvenile literature. I. Title.
F128.64.L6O77 2016
974.7'1—dc23   2015032376

Editorial Credits
Michelle Hasselius, editor; Richard Parker, designer; Wanda Winch, media researcher;
Steve Walker, production specialist

Our very special thanks to Jennifer L. Jones, Chair, Armed Forces Division at the National Museum
of American History, Kenneth E. Behring Center, Smithsonian, for her curatorial review. Capstone
would also like to thank Kealy Gordan, Product Development Manager, and the following at
Smithsonian Enterprises: Ellen Nanney, Licensing Manager; Brigid Ferraro, Vice President, Education
and Consumer Products; Carol LeBlanc, Senior Vice President, Education and Consumer Products.

Photo Credits
Alamy: Image Bank, 21 (right); Architect of the Capitol/John Trumbull, 7 (bottom); By Courtesy of
the Ellis Island Immigration Museum, 4, 14 (right), 16 (left), 18, 20, 21 (left); Corbis, 22; Courtesy,
American Antiquarian Society, 13 (bottom); Granger, NYC, 7 (top), 14 (left), 15, 17, 23 (all); Ian
Brabner, Rare Americana, 13 (top); Library of Congress: Prints and Photographs Division, 9 (top), 10,
11 (all), 12, 16 (right) 19, 25; Newscom: Picture History, 24, Prisma, 26, Zuma Press/Bryan Smith, 27
(bottom); PhotoSpin, 27 (top); Shutterstock: Aeypix, 29, Arevik, paper design, iNaughtyNut, cover,
pisaphotography, 28, Songquan Deng, 9 (bottom), Weerawich, 5; U.S. Patent Office, 8; Wikimedia:
Truchelut, Rue de Grammont, Paris, 6

Printed in the United States of America in North Mankato, Minnesota.
009221CGS16

Table of Contents

Primary Sources

Studying history is like traveling back in time. It shows you how people really lived. People can learn about the past through letters, photos, paintings, or newspaper articles. These are examples of primary sources. Primary sources are created at the time of an event.

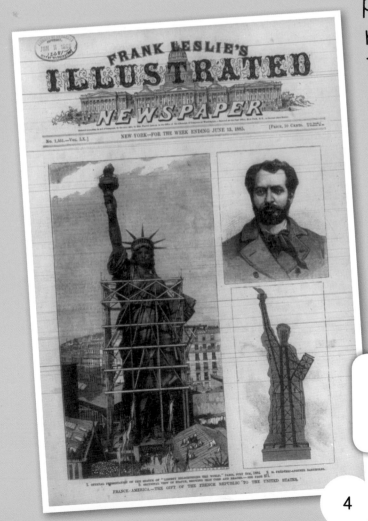

newspaper article from 1885 about building the Statue of Liberty

The Statue of Liberty is also a primary source. This national monument can tell us about history.

the Statue of Liberty

The Statue of Liberty at a Glance

- made out of iron and copper
- looks like Libertas, the Roman goddess of freedom
- also known as Lady Liberty and Liberty Enlightening the World
- 305 feet (93 meters) tall, from the ground to the tip of the torch
- concrete foundation weighs 27,000 tons (24,494 metric tons)
- arrived in the United States in 1886
- located on Liberty Island in New York Harbor

The Two Sisters

portrait of Edouard de Laboulaye

The idea for the Statue of Liberty began at a dinner party in France in 1865. Edouard de Laboulaye was grateful that the United States and France were so close. He called the countries two sisters. Laboulaye also liked that America valued freedom. He wanted France to give their sister country a statue that stood for freedom.

"Wouldn't it be wonderful if people in France gave the United States a great monument as a lasting memorial to independence ..."
—Edouard de Laboulaye

A sculptor named Frederic-Auguste Bartholdi was at the party. He began thinking about how to make the statue.

portrait of Frederic-Auguste Bartholdi in 1886

This painting from 1820 shows the British Army surrendering to French and American forces in 1781.

FACT

During the Revolutionary War (1775–1783), France fought with the American colonies against Great Britain. France helped America win its independence.

An Idea Grows

Bartholdi thought about the statue for years. He drew many pictures of it. He wanted the statue to look like Libertas, the Roman goddess of liberty and freedom. The statue would have a long dress. It would hold a torch.

drawing of the Statue of Liberty on Bartholdi's design patent in 1879

view of New York City and New York Harbor in the 1880s

Bartholdi sailed to New York in 1871. As he came into New York Harbor, he saw an island. It was the perfect spot for the statue.

FACT

The name of the island where the Statue of Liberty stands has changed. In 1956 Bedloe's Island was changed to Liberty Island.

An American Symbol

Bartholdi was not only the statue's sculptor. He was also its salesman. He had to get America to help pay for the statue. He met with many important people, including U.S. President Ulysses S. Grant.

President Ulysses S. Grant around 1870

To help raise money, French builders made the statue's arm and torch first. They were displayed in Philadelphia, Pennsylvania, in 1876.

For 50 cents people could climb up and stand on the torch's balcony. The money went to help build the rest of Lady Liberty.

This photo shows the statue's torch and arm on display at the 1876 Centennial Exposition.

a photo of the exhibits in the main building of the Centennial Exposition in Philadelphia

FACT

The Statue of Liberty's arm was displayed during the Centennial Exposition in Philadelphia. The event celebrated the 100-year anniversary of the Declaration of Independence.

Give, Give, Give

Climbing onto Lady Liberty's arm raised money. But seeing its head raised even more. The Statue of Liberty's head was displayed in Pennsylvania in 1878. More money came in, but it still wasn't enough.

a photo of the Statue of Liberty's head in Paris, France, in 1883

People in America and France had many ideas to raise money. They sold lottery tickets. They made small statues and sold them to children and schools. Finally there was enough money to complete the huge statue.

Building a Giant

Imagine having to make a hand so large, you could stand in it. That was only one piece of the giant statue. Builders worked 10 hours a day, seven days a week for nine years to complete the statue.

completing the statue at the Gaget foundry in Paris in 1883

FACT

Architect Gustave Eiffel made the statue's spine. Eiffel is famous for building the Eiffel Tower in Paris.

a photo of Bartholdi and his workers making a plaster mold of the statue's left hand in 1875

The Statue of Liberty was finished in France in July 1884. But it took another year before it arrived in the United States.

FACT

The Statue of Liberty's index finger is 8 feet (2.4 m) long. That's as tall as two second-graders standing on top of each other!

Coming to America

Bartholdi had to get the statue to Bedloe's Island. But the statue was too big and heavy to travel in one piece. The Statue of Liberty was broken down into 350 pieces. The pieces were packed into 214 crates.

Pieces of the statue arrived in New York in 1885.

a photo taken in 1885 of the statue's feet on Bedloe's Island

For four months the crates sailed across the ocean to Bedloe's Island. But an important piece was still missing. The statue needed a pedestal to stand on.

A Place to Stand

It was America's job to build the statue's pedestal. But raising money for the project was difficult. In his newspaper, *New York World*, publisher Joseph Pulitzer urged citizens to give money to the cause. He helped raise more than $100,000 in six months.

a photo of builders making the pedestal on Bedloe's Island

portrait of Joseph Pulitzer
and his newspaper,
New York World

"We must raise the money! ... Let us not wait for
the millionaires to give us this money. It is not
a gift from the millionaires of France to the
millionaires of America, but a gift of the whole
people of France to the whole people of America."
—Joseph Pulitzer

Give Me Your Tired, Your Poor

American Emma Lazarus wrote a poem called "The New Colossus" in 1883. The poem described the statue as a lady offering a safe place for people coming into the country. The poem was published in two newspapers: *New York World* and *The New York Times*.

portrait of Emma Lazarus

a photo of the poem engraved on the statue

a draft of "The New Colossus," written by Emma Lazarus

In 1903 Lazarus' poem was put on a plaque on the statue's pedestal. It is still there today.

An Invitation to See the Lady

For six months builders used rivets and mallets to hammer pieces of the statue in place. Finally it was time to unveil the Statue of Liberty.

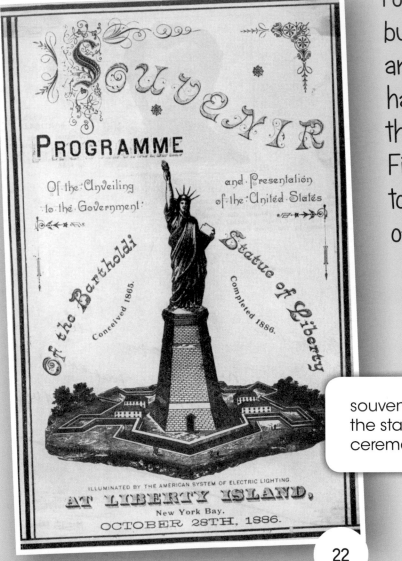

souvenir program from the statue's unveiling ceremony in 1886

an invitation to see President Cleveland accept the Statue of Liberty in New York

On October 28, 1886, people stood on New York City sidewalks to see the statue. President Grover Cleveland gave a speech on Bedloe's Island. He accepted the statue for all Americans.

"... we will not forget that liberty here made her home; nor shall her chosen altar be neglected."
—President Grover Cleveland

Lady Liberty and Ellis Island

New York Harbor has many islands, including the one that holds the Statue of Liberty. Ellis Island is also located in New York Harbor. For more than 60 years, this island was the gateway for millions of people coming to America.

a photo of immigrants looking at the Statue of Liberty as they come to America

immigrants see the Statue of Liberty from Ellis Island in 1930

After 1886 the Statue of Liberty and Ellis Island greeted travelers and immigrants as they arrived in America.

From Lighthouse to National Monument

The Statue of Liberty started out as a lighthouse. The torch's lights could be seen for 24 miles (38.6 kilometers). In 1924 the statue became a national monument. Today millions of tourists come to New York Harbor to see this symbol of freedom.

the Statue of Liberty used as a lighthouse in 1886

a photo of damage on Liberty Island after Hurricane Sandy in 2012

FACT

In October 2012 Hurricane Sandy hit the East Coast and flooded Liberty Island. The Statue of Liberty was closed for eight months to repair the damage.

Timeline

1865   Edouard de Laboulaye comes up with the idea for the Statue of Liberty

1871   Frederic-Auguste Bartholdi sails to New York Harbor and decides to put the Statue of Liberty on Bedloe's Island

1876   The Centennial Exposition displays pieces of the Statue of Liberty for the first time

1883	Emma Lazarus writes "The New Colossus" about the Statue of Liberty
1884	The Statue of Liberty is finished in France
1885	The statue arrives in New York Harbor in 350 pieces
1886	The Statue of Liberty is unveiled on Bedloe's Island
1924	The Statue of Liberty becomes a national monument

Glossary

architect—someone who designs buildings and checks that they are built properly

balcony—a platform with railings on the outside of a building or structure, usually on an upper level

centennial—a 100-year anniversary

colossus—a huge statue or something extremely large

copper—a reddish brown metal; copper turns green over time when exposed to air and water

crate—a large, usually wooden box

immigrant—someone who comes from one country to live permanently in another country

lottery—a game that depends only on chance to win

mallet—a wooden hammer

pedestal—a base for a statue

primary source—an original document

rivet—a short metal fastener or nail

sculptor—a person who makes sculptures by carving and shaping

statue—a model of a person or animal made from metal, wood, stone, or other solid material

symbol—a design or an object that stands for something else

torch—a flaming light that can be carried in the hand

Read More

Gaspar, Joe. *The Statue of Liberty.* American Symbols. New York: PowerKids Press, 2014.

Herrington, Lisa M. *The Statue of Liberty.* Rookie Read-About American Symbols. New York: Children's Press, an imprint of Scholastic Inc., 2014.

Monroe, Tyler. *The Statue of Liberty.* U.S. Symbols. North Mankato, Minn.: Capstone Press, 2014.

Internet Sites

FactHound offers a safe, fun way to find Internet sites related to this book. All of the sites on FactHound have been researched by our staff.

Here's all you do:

Visit *www.facthound.com*

Type in this code: 9781491482230

Super-cool stuff! Check out projects, games and lots more at **www.capstonekids.com**

Critical Thinking Using the Common Core

1. Primary sources are created at the time of an event. Give one example of a primary source. (Key Ideas and Details)

2. The Statue of Liberty was too big and heavy to travel from France to Bedloe's Island. How did Bartholdi get the statue to New York Harbor? (Key Ideas and Details)

3. Immigrants see the Statue of Liberty when they come to America. What does "immigrant" mean? (Craft and Structure)

Index